Summary and Discussions

of

Hoax: Donald Trump, Fox News, and the Dangerous Distortion of Truth

by Brian Stelter

wizer

Disclaimer:

You are viewing a summarization of the chapters and content from the book "Hoax: Donald Trump, Fox News, and the Dangerous Distortion of Truth."

The contents of the summary are not intended to replace the original book. It is meant as a supplement to enhance the reader's understanding. Again, the intention is for this complimentary guide to encourage and inspire the reader to get the full and original book to further their comprehension.

Test Yourself:

1. Whose show seemingly prompted Trump to stop air travel to and from China in the wake of coronavirus?

2. Name three networks called "fake news" by Trump.

3. What source did Stelter first think may have been a plant by Fox?

(Answers at the end of the book.)

Before You Go Any Further,

Download Your Audiobook for Free Now!

Download This First

As a way of saying "Thank You" for your interest in our book, we would like to gift you a surprise random wizer audiobook - 100% Free!

Go to: gowizer.com/free-audiobook

*This is a limited time offer and can expire at any time.

Table of Contents

Test Yourself:.. iii

Download Your Audiobook for Free Now!   iv

Who Should Read "Hoax"?... 1

What's in it for Me & Why is it Important? 2

You'll Soon Discover... 3

Who is Brian Stelter? 4

What is Brian Stelter's Perspective? 6

Overview of "Hoax" 7

Prologue of "Hoax".. 9

Recap of Prologue 16

Chapter 1 of "Hoax": The Creation 18

Recap of Chapter 1 29

Chapter 2 of "Hoax": The Candidate............................ 30

Recap of Chapter 2 37

Chapter 3 of "Hoax": The Commander......................... 38

Recap of Chapter 3 49

Chapter 4 of "Hoax": The Cult 50

Recap of Chapter 4 61

Chapter 5 of "Hoax": The Control Freak....................... 62

Recap of Chapter 5 67

Chapter 6 of "Hoax": The Crisis 68

Recap of Chapter 6 76

Conclusion of "Hoax" 77

Test Yourself on "Hoax" 78

Answers for "Test Yourself" Questions......................... 80

Discussion Questions on "Hoax".................................... 82

Editorial Review of "Hoax" *84*

"Hoax" in a Tweet *86*

About Your Summarizer... **87**

Claim Your Unannounced Bonus...*88*

Who Should Read "Hoax"?

Donald Trump has been a source of media sensationalism and contention from the start of his career and throughout his Presidency. His use of the media to gain talking points has been well documented. In fact, it has led to a single network, Fox News, becoming a Trump-led organization. Whether this was his intention or an accident, it has happened.

This book is perfect for those who:

- Want to better understand the Trump-Fox connection
- Are open-minded enough to consider a viewpoint aside from radical Republican
- Question media bias
- Consider themselves well-informed
- Are preparing to vote in the next election.

What's in it for Me & Why is it Important?

President Trump has been a highly controversial president, but the longer he has been in office, this extreme nature has been exacerbated by Fox News. Fox has softened every blow tossed at the President and spun stories to place blame on others whenever possible. This has not only pushed the news network to the extreme right but made it an addictive source for radical followers. It has also radicalized more people who believe all things promoted on the "opinion" shows for the Fox Network. This extreme form of trust and belief is dangerous to overall democracy.

Individuals need to get information from multiple sources to gain an overall view, even if it is not one with which they agree. This book, written by a reporter for CNN, investigates the Trump-Fox collaboration that was once largely ignored but has been brought to light more with the pending election. It is important to read books like this one for an insider look at what the media does to the public and how that power is yielded.

You'll Soon Discover...

- The power media holds and can use or abuse.

- Why it is important to seek news from multiple networks.

- How ratings drive stories on the media.

- How ingrained Trump is to Fox and vice versa.

- How Fox has created a monster in Trump that can harm democracy.

Who is Brian Stelter?

Brian Stelter is an American political commentator for CNN. As the chief media correspondent and host of *Reliable Sources,* he hopes to offer unbiased media coverage of political matters, including the President. A former media reporter for *The New York Times* and editor of *TVNewser,* he has been in this realm of media for many years. Every Sunday, he goes worldwide for CNN to host stories that are relevant for the week. Additionally, Mr. Stelter writes for a nightly email newsletter to keep people well-informed. As a writer, Stelter's book *Hoax* was released in the Fall of 2020 to help the public understand the connection between the White House, the President, and Fox News. This connection is one that has caused and created great confusion for many.

Brian Stelter has been interested in media and broadcasting for most of his life. This passion has led him to seek the truth about matters in unique ways, supported by his parents, especially his mother, following his father's death. Though times were tough, she supported his growing interest in the internet and sharing opinions,

his take on the facts, and news through his lens. This helped him

achieve what he has become today—an on-air reporter who tries to

get an unbiased, journalistic outlook onto the screens of people

everywhere.

What is Brian Stelter's Perspective?

Brian Stelter is an on-air personality that is committed to journalistic integrity, especially in the political realm. As a host for CNN, Stelter has watched as the Trump Presidency has fed into the success of Fox and vice versa. This is problematic for someone who has watched once mostly unbiased, slightly right reporters turn into mouthpieces for the President. These reporters who once would have asked the tough questions seem to have turned into on-camera radicals who soften every hard-hitting story that could make the President look bad or be viewed negatively. Stelter, who has been verbally attacked by those who support Fox and even some hosts, wants the public to be aware of the dangers to democracy if the President controls the media. That is why this book was written.

Overview of "Hoax"

Hoax: Donald Trump, Fox News, and the Dangerous Distortion of Truth is a book that takes a hard look into the well-known relationship between Fox Network and President Trump. Not only does the President live on a steady diet of Fox News, he often contacts Hannity and others to discuss the programs and rant about given topics. It appears the President even takes his talking points from Fox commentators and vice versa, creating a dangerous loop that has affected numerous Americans. This is especially evident in the current coronavirus crisis that is plaguing the nation.

The intent of the book is not necessarily to undermine Fox or all the changes it has encountered due to the new alliance. The book is intended to show the scary facts of a president taking charge of the media. Even though this may not have been Fox's original intent. Fox has been embroiled in many legal battles since this change has occurred, but it still ranks at the top of the Neilson ratings. This is in part because of the addictive content that is shown repeatedly on

Fox. It draws in viewers and, in a manner of speaking, brainwashes them into radical Republicans. This is dangerous to democracy in several ways.

This book is separated into six chapters, but the timeline remains consistent in sticking with the theme. Included within the pages are several personal accounts from unnamed sources, many from Fox, though few are still employed there. Stelter's interest in media has been long-standing, but his journalistic integrity prompted the writing of this book.

Prologue of "Hoax"

March 26, 2020, was a dark time for the U.S. because there were 1,000 confirmed deaths from coronavirus. The nation needed a leader, but instead, they had President Donald Trump and Sean Hannity. As the day continued, the death toll grew. The largest concentration of deaths was in Trump's hometown, Queens, New York, which was out of beds, and almost out of ventilators. Though the White House said they were hopeful, two young doctors risked their jobs to video the scene inside the hospital, described as "apocalyptic." Many died, barely able to speak their names, and a turning point in the crisis finally happened.

The President did not read the article that was released, bragging he had canceled his subscription. In fact, Trump claimed Fox News was "fake" and "failing" as they often critiqued his administration. Even stars like Hannity, who had downplayed the virus, looked ignorant considering the new information. Many news outlets played the quote by the doctors, but people had been trained not to trust the media. Trump needed Fox and was upset they would spout such rhetoric. Trump depended on Fox to keep his alternate reality intact.

At 5:30 that day, Trump had gone on the news to announce people should relax, this proved of crisis proportions. So, when he was scheduled for a call with Hannity at 9 p.m., Trump was chomping at the bit. His call to Hannity was patched in like any other caller, yet Trump bragged about putting off a call to the Chinese President to call the show. Trump said Hannity had the number one show on television, even though this was a gross exaggeration. The 40-minute chat with Hannity was consequential to the body politic. They proved Trump did not grasp the urgency that America was facing with the pandemic. Trump even expressed doubt about the number of ventilators Cuomo had requested, feeling they were too large. Ultimately, it was because of social distancing by New Yorkers, but Trump's default seems to be disbelief.

Fox ran a short interview with a radiologist, Saphier, who doubled as a commentator. Still, it was run at one in the afternoon where few would see it. She reiterated the shortage of ventilators. Following the interview with Hannity, Trump called to ask how it went. Trump really wanted to know how the interview rated, which was disgraceful since close to 400 Americans would die that day, gasping for air. Trump's focus was grossly misplaced. Trump also asked if his briefings were pulling in viewers. While many were tuning in, it was not for the President, but a concern for their health that kept them watching. This was the typical Trump vs. the Media type conversation that was all too common. Even in the height of the pandemic, Trump grotesquely touted his ratings.

This was, in part, Hannity's fault as he daily fed Trump's ego. If Hannity had been a true friend, he would have told Trump not to discuss ratings and focus on the pandemic and celebrate healthcare workers. This did not happen, and Trump and Hannity brought out the worst in one another. This twisted relationship had a life and death consequence in early 2020, as Trump called the coronavirus a "new hoax" created by the Democrats. Hoax became a favorite word of Trump, mostly in conjunction with Russia and impeachment, but once about COVID-19. This connection led to many downplaying of the virus and did tremendous damage. Hannity went on air to say he had never called the virus a hoax, which was true, but he did worse. Hannity felt the virus was being used to scare people and bludgeon Trump.

Sean Hannity is possibly the most powerful person in the Trump age and feels he controls the Fox channel. Hannity lived well in his Manhattan mansion worth 10.5 million. He had a pool, dock, and private helicopter in a community where there was only one way in and out. Police monitored those coming and going. Hannity wanted to be a radio star in his early days. In fact, he worked at his college radio station, but there is no mention of him on the website. This is because he never graduated from college. His controversial take on the truth about AIDS landed him a hosting job at a right-wing station in Alabama. He met his wife and married, then moved to a larger market in Atlanta, where he yelled about Bill Clinton to anyone who would listen. There, he met Roger Ailes, who needed a Rush Limbaugh type for Fox News. Hannity's life changed with the added prominence of Fox and the larger salary. Hannity is currently the only prime time host who was there for Fox's launch day and still there 25 years later. In 2010, he fought for the right to work from home, and a state-of-the-art studio was created in his mansion so he could do just this.

Hannity was known in the White House as the President's "shadow" chief of staff, but this was a demanding job. It was also a great deal of power to wield. Though Hannity chose the life, in private, he said Trump was a "batshit crazy person." Hannity could never publicly admit this because of his own business model and commitment to the GOP. Hannity was stressed and burned out, gaining weight, and vaping incessantly. Trump spoke with Hannity daily, recommending talking points, and rating his show. Hannity swore no one understood the relationship with Trump, saying he was not as essential as others claimed. When called on the claim, Hannity diverted and used the perch to defend Trump's response to the pandemic.

Though few saw Hannity in the studio, he was known as a nice, generous guy who had done a great deal for staffers. It was hard to square the man they knew in person with what was on television. At the writing of this book in April 2020, there were many reasons why the U.S. was behind in preparations for the pandemic. Some are economic, some cultural, and others are political, but the Trump-Fox loop is one of those big reasons. As the virus spread, Fox downplayed it, and Trump echoed the remarks. The statements were irresponsible at best, yet Fox prepared for work from home and stay-in-place while telling viewers otherwise. The whole time, death rates for the virus soared, and the Network braced for lawsuits over coverage that was less than factual.

Though no one can accurately recount the number of Fox viewers that died or how individual choices can be blamed on the news, Fox failed to minimalize damage to viewers. It is also impossible to know how many Americans died because the

government acted slowly. Still, Fox was feeding information to the

White House. The author has had a front-row seat to the

Trumpification of Fox and is angry that so many viewers have

repeatedly been fed poor advice. As an American, Stelter is

presenting this book, not as a CNN reporter. He is a concerned

citizen worried about factual journalism and free press. This comes

from Stelter's long obsession with the news, starting at age 10.

Through passion and persistence, he made contacts, including

Hannity and others, and became "talent." His on-air time has allowed

him to hear from many at Fox, who said they were aware of the

Trump takeover. Still, no one stopped it, even reporting things

differently from what they saw in real-time. Reporters seemed to be

scared to talk, yet felt "dirty" in reporting incorrectly. Fox

surrendered to Trump. Though frightened, reporters and assistants

spoke with Hannity to get the truth out. Staffers said the Network

had become dangerous to democracy.

Fox is addictive with an identity. It has become a way of life for its viewers. Hardcore viewers rarely seek balanced media, never changing the channel. It is a huge responsibility to carry, especially in the Trump era. Fox felt pressure to please their base, who became radicalized over time. The confidential sources for this book were also confidential sources for Fox in many cases. This is a hypocritical business overall. Fox is, above all, a moneymaker over a new network. Fox was not always reported in such a way. They were formerly "patriotic without being propagandistic." This has changed. The average consumer does not know how instrumental Fox is in leading White House decisions. Media Matters for America, a progressive group led by David Brock, keeps track. Fox does not agree with his findings.

Recap of Prologue

- March of 2020 was a dark time for America as coronavirus took

over the nation.

- Fox is instrumental in leading White house decisions.

- This book is based on being an American, not a reporter for CNN.

- Hannity is a reporter and a nice guy but has questionable integrity

  as far as journalism is concerned.

- Stelter's obsession with media and presentation started at age 10

and continues today.

Chapter 1 of "Hoax": The Creation

Opening with the quote, "everybody can be bought," chapter one takes things back to 1996 when Trump was buying up buildings and beauty pageants. Rupert Murdoch bought Roger Ailes, who would later be a key player in the drama. Murdoch offered a huge sum of money to build a new channel from the ground up in New York City. Ailes was motivated as he wanted the Republican party to win television like Rush Limbaugh was helping it on the radio. He also wanted to show up his old bosses at NBC. At this time, it was thought the newly created MSNBC would rival CNN, not Fox. Both ABC and NBC had established news divisions. Fox was not even on the radar. Still, Ailes prevailed. Many former lieutenants left NBC for the up and coming Fox. Ailes fought the established media in a bold, strong way.

Fox was aired as the "fair and balanced" channel, making others liberal and media biased. In July 1996, Ailes took the stage to announce the name of the new channel, but beforehand, a press release was handed out to reporters. This press release called other outlets "fake news" 20 years before becoming Trump's mantra. He cited the publics' rather poor opinion of the press overall. It seemed watchers felt the journalists were biased and negative. Fox would be the answer to the issue, and Ailes was in charge. He was bold and obnoxious but made for strong headlines.

During this time, Ailes and Trump ran in the same social circles and were good friends. They shared many characteristics, from fear of crime to racist views and a taste for conspiracies. Both also ran their respective businesses as fiefdoms, with praise expected at every turn. Both appreciated public relations either through puff pieces or stabbing a rival in the back. Trump, specifically, saw no difference in P.R. and press with either offering points for his interests. Trump gained attention because he was willing to talk about gossip from the business community and personal feuds. Gossip columnists loved this. Trump caught the attention of bankers who were then willing to hand over money. At times, Trump flouted his own accolades under the name John Barron. This worked him into the *Forbes* 400 list, even though it was nothing more than an alter ego. Once established, Trump dished out info to anyone willing to give anonymity. Hannity was a beneficiary of this.

To this day, if Hannity cites sources, it is most often the President. Hannity borrowed the term "sources" from journalism, yet derided journalism at every turn. Trump too was a hypocrite. Trump often told Americans not to trust anonymous sources being reported on, while serving as one for Hannity. Backing up a bit, when Trump was divorcing Maples and buying the Miss Universe Organization, Ailes was busy building his Network. Hannity and Colmes would air at 9 pm., a slot still held today. Though Ailes had poached Hannity from the radio and cast him as a mild-mannered liberal as opposed to Colmes, it turned out Hannity was a patriot and Colmes the nerd who was being pushed back by Hannity.

Fox was tough on Clinton during impeachment proceedings, but it was during 9/11 that they began to overwhelm CNN. The Ailes-Hannity combination of in your face type patriotism was paying off.

They were moving closer and closer to the right. Ailes ruled through force, having hidden cameras around the building and a network of informants willing to rat out colleagues for less than saintly reasons. Power was openly equated with fear. Even though Ailes did not understand how the web worked, he knew how important an impression was and made sure he was leaving the one he desired. During the Ailes era, Fox was likened to a cult by staffers. When staffers sent in tips to Stelter about Fox, it eventually got back to Ailes, who criticized him and the "anonymous tips." This stopped tips for a short time, but they eventually resumed. With the recommitment to leaking info, Ailes became obsessed with Stelter's blog.

At one point, an intern from Fox was dispatched to spend time with Stelter. Though he thought at one time they were dating, it eventually came out that she was sent to take notes and report back to her bosses. She was to friend him on Facebook and search for anti-Fox rhetoric to trip him up. This demonstrated Ailes' paranoia. Though tactics were upgraded over time, it was obvious Ailes wanted control and would stoop to unethical behavior to get it. Ailes was a powerhouse with influence enough to say he had elected three presidents, which he had a hand in. His media prowess lifted Nixon, Reagan, and George W to the White House. He waved away flatterers and critics because his goal was not control of the Republican Party, but profits.

When Obama was elected in 2008, Alan Colmes disappeared from the picture. He was no longer needed. This was yet another sharp turn to the right for Fox. The Network turned from left-right debates to predominantly lectures. Hannity began to transform the show, that was not his alone, into what we currently know. His nightly anti-Democratic attacks were made for those who distrusted the news. However, Hannity was still second to Bill O'Reilly. Viewers liked O'Reilly's format better, which fostered serious tension between the two. They bad-mouthed one another behind each other's back but rarely spoke. Though neither watched the other's show, they studied ratings obsessively. O'Reilly stood in Hannity's way of being number one.

Television ratings are controlled by Neilson, and this reveals that while other stations are capturing some viewers at key times, Fox has skyrocketing viewership from the hours prior to dawn to well into the night. There are three telltale signs of a network as far as ratings are concerned. First is the total viewership at any specific time. For Fox, this climbs into the millions as soon as daylight hits. This measures both popularity and loyalty. Next comes cumulative viewership. This is a channel's total reach each month. CNN has people that watch for short periods, but Fox has people that watch for long periods. People watching news networks number around 130 million in a given month, meaning cable networks have power when it comes to shaping national discourse. Finally, viewership in the 25 to 54-year-old demographic is important because this is where the money is found. The average Fox viewer is 67 years of age. Hosts like Hannity study these demographics and the related rating multiple times a day.

Like cable newsers, Trump spun the Apprentice ratings to tell a story, even when viewers stopped watching. Even when called out on this, Trump said that people believed what you told them. Inside

of Fox News, the rating obsession is inescapable. This is because they

have been on top for so long, they want to stay there. This is a daily

topic of conversation. Neilson has become an invisible hand pushing

to keep ratings alive. Fox was an anti-Obama favorite as Ailes tried to

keep the progressives from changing the white-male-dominated

country. However, Ailes could show restraint when he wanted, such

as in the Obama birthplace scandal that was prominent on other

networks, but not Fox. The Tea Party was Ailes testing the waters in

Fox's political mobilizing power with Hannity and Beck promoting

related events across the country. This was a precursor to what

would be the Trump quake.

The conventional wisdom at Fox was to be on the offensive

against Democrats, which was more profitable than defense with

Republicans. When guests arrived pre-Obama, things were well

choreographed, but after, it was an attack on those who were not

conservative. The established norms of political punditry were

ignored to make a point. The barbs became personal, and civility

24

tossed aside. Cable news seemed to incite problems, even if they did

not cause the problem originally.

For Juliet Huddy, the Obama years served as a wake-up call

about Fox because it became a constant anti-Obama conversation.

Objectivity was thrown out for all things anti-Obama. This angered

her as the daytime shows were producer-driven and directed. The

talent was expected to stay on script. This led to the realization that

a former Fox and Friends producer shared, "People think he's

(Trump) calling up Fox and Friends and telling us what to say... It's

the opposite. We tell him what to say." On the set of Fox and

Friends, scandals are conceived, and conspiracy theories floated. This

is all fed to Trump.

Before his election, Trump was tested as a guest on Fox and

Friends. The popularity of the interview turned into "Monday

Mornings with Trump," changing American politics completely. This

segment helped Trump gain points with conservatives and received

the nomination for President. Though Trump was only about half a mile away most days, he chose to call into the show to appear much harder to get in touch with, Ailes did not complain. This segment was a foreshadowing of the relationship between Trump and Fox during his Presidency. Fox and Friends were about ratings and outrage, even beyond Trump. They were trained to spout the beliefs Ailes held, even if they did not agree or adhere to such beliefs. Segments were designed to incite certain emotions like hate, fear, and occasionally, love. Hosts were even asked to ask viewers if the segments had the intended effect. Ailes also knew that sex sells and would use attractive women as prominent in stories to keep men watching. Eventually, Ailes' downfall would coincide with Trump's takeover of the right.

Until Trump announced his desire to run for President, many thought it was just a ploy to keep people watching The Apprentice. When the official announcement was made, the launch speech was a T.V. show, much like the rest of his campaign. Trump ultimately positioned himself to fill a void in politics, much like Fox filled a void in the television market. Though Fox initially stepped back from

Trump to let the nominations play out, he stayed in contact with

them for interviews and through live tweets during the show. In a tiff

with rising star Kelly, Trump became enraged that she covered a

story about Ivana and sworn testimony over a rape. This was a week

before the first GOP primary debate of which she was moderating.

The August 6th debate was viewed by millions, and though

Trump was challenged, making Murdoch happy, Ailes was not.

During the debate, Kelly asked the infamous question about Trump's

treatment of women, which gained Ailes' attention quickly. Trump

called Ailes right after the debate and laid into him about not being a

friend. Kelly had only repeated Trump's own words back to him, but

Ailes told her to stop the "female empowerment stuff." Trump went

after Kelly on Twitter, which justified the questions she had posed.

Ailes tried to console Trump, but he also knew Kelly was important

to the Network. He supported his talent personally but did not want

to alienate Trump either. Ailes calmed Trump for a few days, but

then the attacks started again. Kelly's ratings were largely

unaffected, but because of Trump's vitriol, Fox released a statement that called Trump's actions a sick obsession that was below the dignity of a presidential candidate. This version of Fox is long gone.

Trump's narcissism led him to believe he could call the shots and choose questions for the media. Still, his anti-media campaign cast a shadow on freedom of the press worldwide.

Laws were created to suppress investigative reporting. This was slightly ironic since Trump lived for media coverage. He knew Kelly was a rising star as she graced the cover of *Vanity Fair*, but his relationships with media were also volatile. During a *Time* gala, when primaries were underway, Trump actually complimented the author.

Recap of Chapter 1

- Everyone can be bought, including the media.

- Trump, much like the current Fox, spins media to increase ratings.

- Fox has changed over the years into an unrecognizable network of

  opinion over the news.

- Trump needs the media, but also enjoys calling them "fake."

- Trump's anti-media campaign casts a shadow on free press

  worldwide.

Chapter 2 of "Hoax": The Candidate

Though it seems unimaginable now, Murdoch once told Trump to "calm down." However, during the race, he was slowly giving up on the Jeb Bush camp and moving to Trump's side. This was a painful process for someone who had defended Kelly and even tweeted against Trump during the campaign. Also, during the campaign, Trump would watch Fox incessantly to gain talking points against his rivals. He raved to Ailes daily about any slights and asked when Kelly would get in line or when Karl Rove would be terminated. Trump ranted in public, which is when Murdoch told him to "calm down." The truth was Murdoch wanted a relationship with a president for business purposes. He wanted the power to be invited to state dinners and briefings. Trump could do this if he relaxed a bit.

Trump continued to go after Kelly to the ire of Fox executives. Many felt he was out of control, but Trump wanted Kelly to be made an example at Fox. The exec's concerns were hollow because Fox was not only cursing Trump but keeping him on as a frequent guest on many shows, as well as carrying his rallies live on Fox. Trump's campaign was fought on television for the most part. Kelly noticed all the interviews and felt Ailes was doing the bare minimum when it came to truly defending her. Ailes was not sure what more Kelly wanted. He was juggling a dozen stars and Trump, all with huge egos. This was difficult for the man that was "losing it" in his final years, according to ex-employees.

In July of 2016, Gretchen Carlson sued Ailes and affected Trump's presidential race. Carlson exposed Ailes's predatory tactics and created the #MeToo movement. This led to a deep look into others on sets like Bill O'Reilly and Harvey Weinstein, who is now in jail. The lawsuit went back for years, but not everyone was as thoroughly investigated. Doocy had claims against him, but no notes that he was reviewed are found. Ailes undoing was when Carlson found out she could legally record her interactions with him. These were used in court. However, Carlson was not the first to gather evidence against Ailes. When Carlson was fired, she requested her vacation time before signing the papers. As she left the building, she called her legal team, and two weeks later, Ailes was blindsided by a legal filing. Trump was upset, not by the harassment of Carlson, but about the attack on Ailes. He wanted to help. Though a lawyer and P.R. firm were hired, within a week of the Carlson lawsuit, the Murdoch's agreed Ailes had to go. His behavior was too pervasive for him to continue, new acts were uncovered almost hourly. No one could save him.

This all came to a head at the GOP convention in July when Ailes thought he could still get out from under the "attack" by Carlson. When Ailes finally agreed to step down in resignation, Fox execs wondered how long it would be before he launched a rival network. The next day, Tuesday, Ailes joined the Fox 9 a.m. editorial call as nothing had happened. He kept this up until noon when *New York* magazine revealed Kelly had interviewed with a lawyer detailing harassment. This testimony was a guaranteed scandal with nonstop coverage, just like Murdoch wanted. Fellow anchors were angry at Kelly, and she was escorted in and out of the arena. She found a quiet corner and called a friend who had been harassed who was shocked the information had been leaked. She had to co-anchor the convention alongside people who had turned on her. By Wednesday, Ailes had to get the message. Fox had deactivated his badge, and he could not even enter the building. Before signing the release agreement, Ailes called Trump, who cursed his accusers. Ailes said the silver lining was that he could work on the Trump campaign because he was not allowed to go to a competing network. Trump said they would see about the working relationship. Ailes agreed to sign for a 40-million-dollar walkaway and a muzzle, but could still say he advised Murdoch, though this was a lie. This was announced on Thursday and threatened to overshadow Trump's coronation.

Trump's doom and gloom speech was given from the arena saying Americans would no longer hear lies, while he gave misleading statements. The speech sounded like Ailes through and through, but Ailes watched from home, in the dark. Even in the chaos, Fox employees were shocked at the loss of Ailes, uncertain if the Network would survive. The Murdochs agreed Ailes had to go but did not agree on anything else. James wanted to hire a new head from outside, one that would take Fox back to a middle ground with less Hannity. While Rupert and Lachlan were fond of Rhodes as a hire as well, but to change directions now would be "business suicide." They also did not want James near Fox News as he was too far to the left with his wife's beliefs taking the lead. Instead, Rupert Murdoch took Ailes' place temporarily. He learned Ailes had kept fixers and yes-men on the payroll at Fox, much like Trump. Other instances of unnecessary people were found too, but Rupert cleaned house. In mid-August, Rupert named Bill Shine and Jack Abernathy copresidents, reporting to him. One rung lower were two other Ailes supporters, Jay Wallace and Suzanne Scott. They would report to Shine. All four appointees were Fox News originals. Over the next year, Shine's name came up in conjunction with the lawsuit and misconduct, but Rupert was undeterred.

For Hannity, Trump served for renewed relevance because the previous eight years had been repetitive Obama bashing. Hannity's show had become boring, and producers knew it. Trump, however, was the most interesting story of the decade. Trump listened to Hannity daily, taking his talking points from him, both

men were left unchecked and following their worst instincts. Hannity

prompted Trump to talk on his show and let him speak without proof

or follow-up. When Stelter called Hannity out, the response was

irresponsible at best. Hannity claimed he valued honesty but used

misleading information to promote otherwise.

At the same time, Kelly had a decision to make. With her

contract opened, she was courted by several networks. Though she

stalled for a while, she was hated at Fox by many and chose to leave.

At the same time, there was a suspected alliance between Trump

and Ailes, but the fact was, Trump did not need him, nor did Fox. The

Network kept moving forward, and so did Trump. As far as Fox was

concerned, they kept a profitable business moving forward. Even

Ailes had been replaceable.

Trump had taken over as far as television was concerned, and

Fox helped by pairing Clinton's words and emails together right

before the election. Right after Ailes resigned and before Trump won, just for a moment, Fox News could have changed to a more truth-based format. If Shep Smith had taken over, this might have happened, but after Trump was elected, this was not an option. Fox had expected Clinton to win, but this did not happen, and Hannity's views would reign on air. Even Trump seemed to assume he would lose. Still, when the individual votes were counted, Trump was declared the winner, first on Fox. It all seemed surreal, but it was a great news night.

With Trump elected, he needed to assemble an administration, so he turned to those he knew the best, Fox personalities. This is when the revolving door truly began to spin between Trump and Fox. Those appointed to Trump's team could no longer work for Fox, at least on the payroll, as the social contract was already being established. When O'Reilly took a couple strong-armed jabs at Kelly on air, she made a choice to leave Fox for good. Within a few months, she had a deal with NBC. Kelly was just one of the first journalists to leave Fox during the Trump era.

Recap of Chapter 2

- Trump had an odd obsession with attacking Kelly early on in his

    Presidency.

- Hannity needed Trump to renew interest in his career after eight

    years of anti-Obama rhetoric.

- Trump did not outright control hiring and firing at Fox, but was

    highly influential.

- Trump and Fox created a revolving door between the Network and

    White House.

- Trump ran on the idea America was being lied to, but he also lied.

Are you enjoying the book so far?

If so, please help me reach more readers by taking 30 seconds to

write just a few words on Amazon

Or, you can choose to leave one later...

Chapter 3 of "Hoax": The Commander

Despite all the pandemic era talk of togetherness, there is a divide between the liberal and conservative base. Fox and Trump work to exacerbate those differences often. Fox seemed to enhance fears conservatives already held, and with Trump's win, they felt power was being gained. Fox began to feel like the home team with Trump's shocking victory. While still serving as President-elect in 2017, Trump seized on the phrase "fake news." Though originally intended to refer to clickbait, Trump used it to describe news that should not be believed.

Though Trump built his foundation on "fake news" as a slogan of sorts, it fueled Fox's business model even before Trump became President. Fox was credited with causing conservatists to move to the extreme right before Trump and continues to be given this credit today. Many conservatives refuse to listen to anything not vetted through Fox. They have become the gospel as far as politics are concerned. This became dangerous during the coronavirus outbreak. This is because the President and Hannity were telling conservatives to only trust Fox, yet reporting un-news. This cycle continued to alienate traditional news sources and create an authoritarian approach in a country known for the freest press in the world.

From the beginning, Trump would say anything he felt, even if it was not factual. He needed his two Seans, Hannity and Spicer, to do the same from their platforms. The chaos started the Saturday after the inauguration. An early morning news report said Trump's crowd was smaller than Obama's had been. This was factual reporting, and while it was a small story for the day, Trump took offense and became obsessed. This set the stage for all of Trump's Presidency as he called Fox to complain. Overall, discussions of journalism in the age of "alternative facts" lit up the newsroom in the early Trump days. Dealing with the lies coming from the White House and misinformation would stay a hot topic for most networks, but not Fox.

In most cases, Fox reported the opposite of other networks. Some may call this contrarian or a cover-up, but for the Murdoch's, it was pure business and a ratings boost. From the outside, the result was inexcusable and treachery. This trend continued through to 2020. Though much of what came out of Trump's mouth was inaccurate or illogical, Fox took his words at face value. His failures were treated with kid gloves and lies were totally ignored. For Hannity, this was easy as he believed no matter what, "Democrats are worse." To explain this, Fox staffers said that they had no real leadership after Ailes, and while Fox was originally produced for Ailes, it was now designed for Trump. This was shown when Earhardt was taken into the Trump administration, giving up her job at Fox.

The President's first-time using *Fox & Friends* for talking points was a week into his Presidency. This was over a story in which Chelsea Manning was released after a 35-year sentence. Still, Trump misheard or misread the report on television captioning. He tweeted about her being a traitor, which was unrelated and caught by Stelter, who alerted the original reporter. Still, the producers of *Fox &*

Friends did not make sure the President was well informed or even accurate. He and they were allowed to rip stories off right-wing blogs, play to conspiracy theories, and take the easy path. Trump made policy decisions based on random T.V. pundits, and they ate up the power.

Over time, tweet by tweet, the country began to understand that the President's statements were misinformed. No one stopped the President, even though several should have made an effort. Most chalked this up to Trump being elected, and as President could choose to believe and share what he chose. It was not long for anchors like Hannity, Doocy, and Pirro to realize that they had the power to make a policy impact for Trump from the anchor desk. Stories were chosen, knowing Trump would be watching. This was at strong odds with journalistic values. However, those who catered to Trump were promoted, and those who stayed on the sidelines were left on the sidelines. Childers was one who was left where she started because she would not totally cater to Trump.

Some at Fox missed Ailes, feeling he would have organized differently. One well-known name (withheld) felt O'Reilly would have been good for America as well. Though O'Reilly had not been well-liked, he would have been honest about everything. Though O'Reilly partially supported and even hung out with Trump, he was not afraid to make him angry. This was in opposition to Hannity, who catered to Trump. O'Reilly, in an interview with Trump just days before the Superbowl, questioned him about his friendship with Putin. Trump said it was better to get along with Russia than not, which opened the door to further questions. Still, O'Reilly backed off, never really getting answers though he could have pushed further. The sound bite helped Russian propaganda and hurt Trump's standing, yet the White House made no statement to get ahead of the release. The media war was in full effect. Those who worked for Fox supported Trump and stayed on board, always promoting the idea that other news outlets lied. Trump reinforced this at every turn. The irony was that though Trump seemingly hated the media, he also pined for their attention.

One Fox original, Campaign Cameron, left when his contract ran out in 2017. He was at Fox from the beginning, and while he remained steadfast in his beliefs to report the news, the station changed around him. He refused to bow to Trump, so when his contract ran out in 2017, he walked away with his second wife. He watched as the Network adopted a more aggressive approach over time, focusing on opinion over the news. It became more about entertainment than reporting. Cameron repeatedly voiced concerns while Trump's campaign was ongoing. He was required, though not specifically asked, to scrub his opinions from the script, to keep his job. Cameron felt that Trump's "showmanship buffoonery" was addictive for the masses; journalists were just there to listen. Cameron admits that the campaign coverage on Trump, including that on Fox, was toughest on Trump. Still, Trump wanted to be remembered, and he was; everything else was absorbed. Cameron's dedication to the truth was shared by many behind the scenes persons at Fox. They understood that every time talent got on camera and shared incorrect stories or said real journalism was dead that they were undermined and insulted. While several complained, they were advised to focus on their own shows. Fox was split between those reporting the news and those with "shows." This divide would only expand over time.

Reporters such as Baier, Wallace, and Shep continued to work from the inside, preserving some space for news as Hannity and Trump gained power at the Network. This continued over time with stories about Obama bugging the White House, presented as fact, but unvetted and was a long-standing Trump-era conundrum, "Trump was right, Obama did it" commentary. Eventually, with the onslaught of a new lawsuit, O'Reilly was also ousted, but he was given a parting gift of 25 million dollars without getting a chance to say goodbye. Trump, as he had previously had supported O'Reilly, but when he was fired, Trump moved on. Trump still needed the Fox Network, but he did not need any one individual. Next on Trump's list was the new, biggest star, Hannity.

Hannity embraced his newfound position on the top and took advantage of his access to the President. He was coasting, even giving time to O'Reilly on first his broadcast, then his radio show

when Fox refused further interviews. Many felt it sent the wrong

message to female staffers. While Hannity enjoyed the privileges of

being close to the President, it was also exhausting as his rants and

ravings were hard work. As Hannity enjoyed being popular with the

President, as several others at Fox did as well, things for Shine were

not going well. Several lawsuits against him were point to his firing.

Hannity threatened to walk with him, but a week later, when Shine

was "whacked" or fired, Hannity assured the staff he was staying. He

was the number one rated person on the number one network. He

had nowhere to go. Even though he did not leave, Hannity lobbied

with Trump to hire Shine on staff.

Bolling was given Shine's time slot, and some felt it was

because he was one of Trump's top boosters. However, two days

before the show, two female cohosts were added, making him a part

of a trio. The show was canceled within months. Producer Suzanne

Scott seemed to dodge all blame for the failure and was in line to be

Fox's first-ever female CEO. Scott was known as the wardrobe enforcer, delivering what Ailes had demanded previously. Scott was not well-liked by staff or talent, but she rose in the ranks. She was out of her league, according to colleagues, but Ailes had liked her, and so did those who followed him.

Speaking of Ailes, during this time, he had moved to Florida in a 36-million-dollar home because Florida courts could not force a home sale to pay for judgments, and he owed plenty. He had lost touch with Trump but knew Rupert had his ear. Though Ailes had an idea to help create a new network, before discussing the possibility, a fall in his bathroom caused him enormous damage. He died from related issues. Despite his views, faults, and flaws, many on Fox mourned the loss publicly on air. Shep signed off with the following tribute, "To the true victims, respect, and comfort. It's all so complicated. Everything here was and is, as he was." In his will, Ailes left a quarter million for his brother, 100 thousand for a former bodyguard, and 30 thousand to former assistant Judy Laterza, with the rest going to his wife and son. His funeral looked like a Fox news event with Hannity, Ingraham, Hemmer, and Guilfoyle in the front row. They mourned his death, but also the Roger rule at Fox. Trump never called with condolences.

Before Ailes' death, Trump fired Comey, and chaos streaked through Washington. Trump told Sessions, "This is the end of my presidency, I'm fucked" when Mueller was let in. Trump was wrong because he still had Fox and Hannity. Ailes may be gone, but the troops knew what to do. Mueller became the new target, an enemy to Fox viewers. Still, viewers knew the Trump Presidency was in danger. Fox fell to the third ranking, and the Murdoch's knew they were in trouble. With money on the line, Fox's top shows responded with "deny, downplay, and distract." Though wrongful facts were claimed, it did not matter. This continued in the story of Rich, the alleged whistleblower who was killed, even after the idea was proven false. Fox was falling fast, and Hannity was steering. It seemed he could not be stopped. There were no checks and balances in place for Fox. This continued with Trump listening to the news and often repeating, without fact-checking, erroneous material. Hannity was always quick with the cover-up and redirection. Rupert Murdoch was also at Trump's right hand, often receiving calls from him. By mid-2020, there were at least 20 known instances of people moving from Fox to Trump and the White House.

By late 2017, America was suffering in a big part of Trump's response to Charlottesville. He seemed to support Nazis and Klansmen, which turned the stomachs of Democrats and Republicans alike. Several big names left Fox before their contracts ended because of the way Fox spun the story. Concern over Trump's mental health was growing. Still, Fox persisted. Rupert and Scott made adjustments to place Hannity in the coveted 9 p.m. slot to hold up Fox and its lineup in association with Trump. Hannity agreed to do most shows live, though he preferred pre-taping. Ingraham took his 10 p.m. slot, and Bream was rewarded with the 11 o'clock spot. These were the people who offered Trump shelter from the storm when he so often needed it. Many of Fox's holding was sold to Disney, but Fox News was held back for one Murdoch son to run. However, it was a disappointment to the sons. It ended a long family drama, and the Fox-Trump union was left intact.

Recap of Chapter 3

- Liberal and conservative bases have been divided completely by

  Trump and Fox.

- America has suffered at Trump's hand and because of his

  leadership.

- Ailes once felt he was irreplaceable, but once he resigned, this was

  proven wrong.

- Ailes' death did not mean his memory did not loom over Fox.

- Trump felt he would be impeached.

Chapter 4 of "Hoax": The Cult

As Trump's Presidency progressed, a coordinated campaign against him intensified. The "Fake Freak" and "You're not Making America Great" were common taglines. This only intensified with time. Fox's truthtellers faced attacks because they were considered turncoats. One, Neil Cavuto, read the hate mail on air. Though not a supporter of Trump, Cavuto told haters to focus the attention where it belonged, on Trump's worst enemy, himself. Trump tended to contradict himself and flounder. He could lie to your face but did not believe he was lying.

Trump was often slipped rating sheets so he would interview for certain shows. In his mind, this was also an ego boost as if Fox doing well meant he was doing well. After the first year, Trump's interviews lost the pull, and he literally started phoning it in. The only thing that drew a crowd was when he blurted out inappropriate comments on air. Though aides tried to intervene, they could only say "no" so often. More than once in the next year, Trump phoned into *Fox & Friends* and basically took over the show, having to be cut

off when time ran out. The "Friends" were usually easy on Trump,

and he was the first President in history to receive such treatment.

Fox egged on the treatment by hiring more pro-Trump supporters

and creating "feel-good" segments in towns where Trump's support

was well known. There were stories online about families torn apart

by a loved one's addiction to Fox News, but it continued.

One veteran staffer at Fox said, "I feel like Fox is being held

hostage by its audience." Any momentary break from talking about

Trump was penalized by the audience switching stations or

complaining online. It was all about being with or against Trump.

Stelter often received tweets and hate mail directed to him

personally from Trump supporters who were shocked when he

responded. Shep, who worked at Fox in the 3 p.m. slot, had been

outed by the Network, though he never hid his being gay. Still, on an

anti-gay network, this caused some issues in the public eye. He also

stood for truth over bowing to Trump's whims, which caused him to

be largely disliked. When given a chance to quit, he refused, afraid of what would happen to the Network if some truth was not in the mix.

He signed on with a nice bonus but spent as little time as possible at

headquarters. He missed the days of everyone getting along, but also

enjoyed what he was doing. In private, he blamed Trump and felt

Hannity sold out.

When it came out that Hannity had connections to Cohen,

Trump's lawyer, who had helped hide women related issues, Shep

broke the news. Though Fox tried to cover it up, it was eventually

released that it was mostly over real estate deals. The Network

continued to support Hannity wholeheartedly. The irony is that those

"elite" media types he spoke out against actually described him. In

May of 2018, Scott was promoted to CEO, a historic move for Fox

that had never had a female in that position and because it meant

right-wing opinion was winning while the news was losing out. The

same day, Jay Wallace was also promoted to serve as President

under Scott. Scott was preferential toward "programming," so that is

what took precedence. Scott and Wallace disagreed on this point,

but she had a bit more power. Shep tried to maintain the wall between news and opinion, but a rising star, Ed Henry, was breaking through that wall.

As time went on, Hannity earned a nickname, "Shadow Chief of Staff." This was used both in the White House and in *The Washington Post*. The fun-loving Hannity disappeared, and the stress of counseling Trump at all hours was wearing on him. While he was all smiles when with Trump, he felt like he offered advice that was never taken. It was intense work with questionable appropriateness. As the stress got more intense, Hannity lobbied harder to get Shine hired to calm the constant calls.

In June 2018, Hannity flew to Singapore for the summit between Trump and Kim Jong Un, where host Abby Huntsman accidentally called POTUS a dictator. Though Fox did not notice, Twitter erupted with laughter. Hannity landed the after-summit interview and tried to spin it to Trump's favor. Hannity could actually stop Trump from making news and stick to his favorite lines and lies. Though Trump sometimes mocked Hannity for low-quality questions, he kept allowing himself to be interviewed. After the interview with Hannity, Trump had a press conference with real reporters and questions. The reporters questioned his source of power, and Trump did nothing to hide it; it was Fox News and the media. Trump continued to create scandal several times each day, keeping the media busy.

When the story of children being separated from parents crossing the border, then being caged broke, it was Huntsman who broke the Fox code and interjected her opinion. She could not stick to the Trump talking points any longer. She had been in talks with ABC execs but was reluctant to make a move until that moment. She walked away. Still, many who disagreed stayed, and Stelter was asked about this often. No one understood why. Hannity was the face of Fox News and indulged in conspiracy theories as Fox turned a blind eye to Trump's obvious hypocrisy. Why did more people not jump ship? The answer is that some had full devotion to Trump, but for others, it was all about the money. There was also a sense of family at Fox who took care of anchors and employees who were having a tough time. When needed, new protections were put into place for employees. When an anchor and his family were in an accident, Fox offered to send a private jet to get them home. New, huge offices and a new newsroom were also an incentive. The money would not be matched or upped elsewhere.

In July of 2018, Trump hired Shine at Hannity's insistence. Shine became deputy chief of staff. His first assignment was coverage of the Kavanaugh confirmation hearing. This was a point of contention as Fox ran the story, and it made Kavanaugh appear impartial. Other networks felt he could not be both impartial and also use Fox as a platform. Following the Kavanaugh hearing and an attack on Fox about him, Trump found a new meaning for the term "hoax." This term was now used in conjunction with fake news and witch hunt, changing the language of politics. Everyone was expected to choose a side, pro- or anti-Trump. Institutional trust was low and falling among Republicans due to innumerable reasons. Trump's media allies worked to convince people that he was not so bad because everyone was a liar, but Trump was on their side. Trump led a hate movement against media outlets that did not support him, but no one called him out. He was a hypocrite and dangerous, but loyalists were rewarded.

Hope Hicks was hired at Fox and was largely unprepared for the job. Her first announcement was corporate (Fox) support for the First Step Act. The Trump-Fox alliance was so strong that even Bill Shine had a soft landing and was on Fox's payroll for two years after going to work for Trump. This was part of his 7-million-dollar severance package. Trump soon soured on Shine but placed him on the reelection campaign. Guilfoyle also got a soft landing when being outed from Fox. She had several H.R. complaints, mostly by women, about being too open about her sex life. She knew her exit date, though it was not publicized and suddenly began dating Donald Jr, just as his divorce was being finalized. She had Trump push to keep her on the air until the last moment. She was ousted and went on the campaign trail with Donald Jr., hosting streaming video shows. She was not missed at Fox, yet she attended interviews with Donald

Jr when he was interviewed at Fox. This appeared desperate to some.

Once unbound from the truth, Fox could report on whatever it deemed fit. It could also ignore what it wanted. Hannity fed into the irrationality claiming Obama led a plot against getting Trump elected. Hannity and Trump were highly aligned, but Hannity denied giving Trump a sneak peek at monologues. The truth was the information came from Trump's "Executive Time," in which he watched the news and talked to Hannity. This time was extended as the years went on. Trump once said he did not watch television often, but he did so almost constantly. Trump continued to share misinformation throughout the midterms, which incited further hatred for immigrants among his supporters. Only Shep, on Fox, tried to correct Trump, but it did little to stop the lies. News anchors at Fox hated the prime-time crusaders, but not knowing what they were claiming was irresponsible at best.

White identity politics ran rampant at Fox, whether they admitted it or not. Numerous segments preyed on those with racial anxieties over losing white privilege. In all fairness, though, Fox had these types of segments pre-Trump-era politics; they were just extended and more frequent. Fox used headlines about America changing rapidly or the one we knew not existing anymore. Media Matters flagged Fox on Twitter for an anti-immigrant rant, which Fox hated. However, Media Matters felt Fox was causing problems in the country. Fox execs blamed Media Matters for being part of the DNC trying to ruin the Network. Ingraham had made the comment that had everyone up in arms, but she insisted it had not been about race. Other Fox hosts distanced themselves from Ingraham and Carlson, saying they wished the white supremacist stuff would be stopped. Fox talent was allowed to do what they pleased as long as it was right-wing. The management was not strong enough to stop them.

Hannity, still a strong proponent of the President, was overstepping his bounds at every turn. He was considered a special guest at a Presidential rally and asked on stage. This made it appear he was campaigning for Trump, which was not allowed by the press. Though he denied the accusation, he did take the stage at Trump's prompting and call the "people in the back" fake news, insulting his coworkers from Fox, who were seated with the press. Hannity was becoming an embarrassment to his coworkers, yet Fox was allowing him to speak largely unchecked. Scott assured the rest of the staff that such a thing would never happen again, but few believed in her power to stop Hannity. She did offer a weak, nonspecific reprimand, but this did little to appease the "news" section of Fox, and though Hannity was not named, he did refuse to appear on a prime time show he was slated to do. They persisted, and other networks felt Fox had inside information. While Hannity may have, the news side of things was often left out of the loop, getting stories behind other networks.

As testimony came out and the Mueller noose started tightening, Fox talk shows reverted to the "invasion" of immigrant's story that had been blown up in past shows. Then the news turned to Trump fighting for border wall funds to complete his campaign promise. He needed money or would close down the government, but then gave in almost immediately. When Trump supporters showed outrage, Trump took a stand, and the government did shut down, but only temporarily. Again, Trump caved, and the government opened back up 19 days later. Many networks reported the giving in, but Fox spun the President's line as always.

Peters, a ten-year veteran of Fox and staunch Republican, hated Obama but was not impressed with Trump either. In March 2018, he was so angered over the way Trump fed into Fox and vice versa, he wrote a scathing letter calling his colleague's amoral prostitutes for the President. He wrote that Trump was a "danger to the republic." Peters further condemned Fox's core fans, calling them "couch-potato anarchists." This was all said publicly to the surprise of many, but he was not the only one who felt this way. Many others shared the view but lacked financial security to leave their jobs. The Fox of the past, though right-leaning, was gone and had totally fallen over to the right. One on one, even Carlson, Hannity, and Ingraham will not defend Trump, taking an anti-

Democrat view over a pro-Trump viewpoint. However, over time,

Fox went from news reporting to propaganda. This propaganda

worked, and viewers believed Trump in what he said because

Hannity offered support.

Recap of Chapter 4

- Those who stayed tied to the truth instead of Trump were

considered turncoats at Fox.

- The Trump-led Network lost many staffers and veterans of the

  Network because of the changes in fact-checking.

- The Fox network failed to support reporters Trump openly attacked

online.

- Hannity continually overstepped the line when it came to

supporting Trump.

- Fox's core fans were called "couch potato anarchists."

Chapter 5 of "Hoax": The Control Freak

When Democrats took control of the House after the 2018 midterms, Fox considered it a win because they had an enemy served up on a platter. Fox preferred the opposition approach. The emergence of AOC (Alexandria Ocasio-Cortez) and the New Green Deal were gifts for Fox. The previous delineation between news and opinion was coming down at Fox, which was accepted, but problematic. Viewers wanted to hear someone who agreed with them, but Fox wanted to be a top news network, not an opinion network. This caused tension. When DNC chair Tom Perez banned Fox from the debate process, after much prompting, Democrats began to ask again if Fox was a legitimate news network given their strong ties to Trump.

Some Democrats refused to appear on Fox, while others felt appearing was the only way to make a difference. Those who pushed for appearances wanted Democrats to be defined by actual

Democrats, not Hannity and Tucker. On March 8th, Shine resigned as

Trump's communication director. Though it played as a difficult

decision in the media, it was not Shine that was the problem, but

Trump, who needed to improve as President to get better media.

Still, over time Trump supported those at Fox who spoke out "for our

country" instead of remaining politically correct. When "Justice

Jeanine" got in trouble for refusing to apologize for a rant and

suspended, Trump tweeted that she should be welcomed back. He

wanted those that played to his ideas on air, but lost advertising was

pushing Fox to take action.

Amid all the chaos and even vitriol pointed in his direction,

Shep served as the backbone of Fox. Many at Fox thought about

leaving, but job openings for former Fox employees were scarce with

few exceptions. Fox had tainted their careers in irrefutable ways.

Trump was allowed to continue spreading his falsehoods through

Twitter and on-air at Fox, but this was not the Murdoch's stuck in a

hard spot because they had chosen to place themselves there. The

opponents were numerous inside, and outside of Fox, the ratings were there, so it continued. When Trump attacked the reporters of Fox for not fully supporting him, Shep pressured Scott to put out a statement rebuking the President, but she refused. This created negative morale among those attacked and allowed Trump to continue.

Trump continued to be emboldened by Fox's playing dumb and spoke out more against accurate reporting from the station. Still, those that helped encourage Trump at Fox used the association for their personal agendas. Ingraham put the pressure on for the wall. Levin urged Trump to destroy the FISC. Dobbs wanted him to crush China, and Hegseth wanted pardons for military members accused of war crimes. Carlson pushed against aggressive action in Syria and Iran and was actually credited with stopping Trump from bombing. While, to his credit, Carlson never called POTUS, though Trump often called him. Hannity, on the other hand, called Trump personally. However, Fox repeatedly denied being "Trump's network" because every show was different. Still, if you were someone at Fox, it seemed to be because the President tweeted about your show.

Correspondents at Fox suffered because it was easier to create conflict than cover real stories. Management left the news in neutral, rarely showcasing featured stories. Instead, they showed preference to "personalities and pundits." Over time, this played on Shep, who did his hour and then withdrew. Colleagues noticed, so did family and friends. He seemed to run hot and cold. Ailes had been able to keep him on track, but with Ailes dead and Trump hiding any shared truth, Shep felt vulnerable. This showed on his show as his anger overflowed. Barely a year into his new contract, Shep called his agent and said he wanted out. He could no longer stand working at a "state-run" T.V. network. Though Fox was not technically state-run, Trump often talked about Fox like it was. Trump talked up Trump though he felt it could be better if anchors would avoid interviewing his Democratic rivals. Still, Trump had a whiplash-type relationship with Fox. He would call them out one second and call on them the next for attention. Murdoch tended to ignore the attacks but was shocked by the paradox.

In September, Trump was embroiled in the Ukraine scandal. Impeachment seemed inevitable, but Fox was ready to spin the narrative onto the whistleblower instead of Trump. Shep was outraged when a judge was allowed to be called a fool on-air without repercussion. This was the final straw, and for weeks, he and his lawyer worked to undo his contract. Though Fox begged him to stay and basically suck it up, he was done. The ultimate decision went to the top, Robert Murdoch, who said if Shep did not want to work there, he could be replaced. Shep was free to go. On October 11, 2019, Shep signed off for the last time with the words, "Even in our current polarized nation, it is my hope that the facts will win the day, that the truth will always matter, that journalism and journalists will thrive. I'm Shepard Smith, Fox News, New York." This exit was shocking for many and the end of an era for Fox, yet it was symbolic of what was happening to America.

Shep leaving caused turmoil for the reporters left behind. Many questioned whether they should stay. Following Shep's decision to leave, which many questioned as prompted by the

President's clout, Herridge also left, and Barber gave notice.

Ultimately, Shep was replaced by an on-air veteran who was

conservative personally and easy on Trump on air. Hemmer was not

who others hoped would replace Shep, but it was a Fox move further

to the right.

Recap of Chapter 5

- AOC and the New Green Deal were perfect enemies for Fox, who

    preferred the opposition approach.

- When Shep left Fox, it was because of the changing values of the

station.

- Hannity was considered Fox's backbone, though he was moving

ever to the right.

- Fox was showing preference to "personalities over pundits," which

    led to many leaving the station.

- An era ended at Fox, just as it ended for America when Trump

became President.

Chapter 6 of "Hoax": The Crisis

The final chapter begins in the White House, where Dr. Fiona Hill said the T.V. was always on and was typically tuned to Fox News for Trump to watch. It was clear disinformation was being disseminated, and Trump was listening, but no one seemed to be able to stop it. Fox supporters believed every word, and Democrats were highly demonized. The final impeachment vote was at hand on December 18, and Baier said that after that day, "We will never talk about the 45th President of the United States the same way." Everyone expected impeachment. Hannity had other ideas because he knew millions of Trump fans would be glued to his show, but he had family obligations that evening. Hannity pre-taped his show, and though millions thought and expected it to be live, it was not. He was only allowed to do this because no one would stand up and say, "No." This was a disgrace to those reporting live, but Fox did not care as long as the rating stayed up.

Ever since the impeachment was first discussed as a way to remedy misconduct on Trump's part, experts had considered the Fox factor. As the drama unfolded, many who consulted or worked for Fox made the jump to defend Trump. Ultimately, the impeachment trial came down to the strategy that Maureen Dowd summed up as "The Democrats are relying on facts, but the Republicans are relying on Fox." In February of 2020, Republicans in the Senate acquitted Trump on both counts. One Democratic senator, Sherrod Brown, said he saw fear in Republican counterparts. This fear was of Fox and talk radio, as well as of the President. The sole Republican dissenter, Romney, gave an interview about his decision. He said he knew the consequences of his choice, but it was the right choice to make. Trump too gave a single interview to Hannity. The Trump interview was mere propaganda with no real news reported.

When Stelter received an unexpected email from a news researcher new to Fox named Sean Graf, he did not take it seriously. It could have been a trap that was too good to be true. If it was a trap, he would be discredited on Fox. Still, Graf checked out. He had joined Fox in 2016 after striking out at other networks. A known

liberal, he wanted to understand how conservative media worked

from the inside. What he found was that though many within the

organization disagreed with the lack of fact-checking, it was a losing

battle. He said many of the Republicans at Fox were not Trump fans,

and Fox had abandoned the principles they held only a few years

prior. Graf described a business model that depended on Fox's

wingmen, not researched work. The allegiance to Trump was putting

democracy at risk. Graf further commented, "Even if the Republican

Party refuses to stand up to Trump, Fox must." While sympathizing,

Stelter knew that version of Fox no longer existed. Viewers were

radicalized to the point that propaganda was all they craved.

Republicans were changing, and Fox was allowing an

obviously un-conservative President to masquerade as one.

Shamelessness was everywhere, with people expected to pick sides.

Graf left Fox in 2020. In January of 2020, Maria Bartiromo asked

Trump if we should worry about coronavirus. China had only

reported 17 deaths, and most Americans were still in the dark.

Trump was focused on the impeachment trial and domestic concerns. And when for the second time, Alex Azar tried to bring the virus to the President's attention, Trump told him to stop panicking. Wuhan closed down, and America began to evacuate citizens from the area. In the face of all evidence, Trump maintained this position until March, as did most of Fox.

The FCC was contacted saying Fox had blood on its hands because of reports there was no need to panic. Sean Hannity had said the threat was overstated, and many believed. Finally, the President took notice when Fox started offering ideas. Four days after a banner on *Tucker Carlson Tonight* said it was time to stop China flights, the President did just that. With the new restrictions, Trump claimed to have basically shut the virus down. Still, there were new outbreaks in Italy and other areas. Trump ignored experts who pushed for other flight restrictions and a need for more ventilators. Trump even ignored Carlson's televised alerts. Trump, in February, told Trish Regan that China would have it under control by April because hot weather killed the virus. This may be the saddest falsehood in history. If this were true, hundreds of thousands of people might still be alive. Trump seemed to ignore the lack of precaution taking and instead focused on post-impeachment purging at the White House. Fox and the President continued to tell people not to worry even though many were sick and dying.

This continued for the next few weeks with Trump and Fox spinning the virus as under control or being weaponized by Democrats to hurt Trump. Warnings were sounded on other networks, but Fox seemed to silence them. Hannity and Trump had the greatest voices, and they were urging people to ignore concerns over the virus. This was beyond dangerous, but they were not alone in sharing the blame—Fox studios prepared for the impending shutdown well ahead of what they were sharing with viewers. Precautions were taken to keep the news on even if the city shut down, additional building cleanings were added, and hand sanitizer stations were placed by every door. Still, Hannity and other Fox stars spoke out of both sides of their mouths. Aides tried to get Trump to understand the threat, but he would not. That is why Tucker Carlson was called in to talk to Trump. Though Carlson holds no real power, he felt he had a moral obligation to talk to Trump. Discreetly, Carlson tried to get in to see the President at Mar-a-Lago, but he found himself there during a birthday party. When Carlson did get time alone with the President, he tried to explain the virus was beyond containment, and the administration and Fox had failed everyone. This had little effect on Trump, and several members who attended the party came down ill within a week.

On Monday the 9th, Regan's show equated the coronavirus with an impeachment scam. This would be the week everything changed for Americans. Regan was sticking with the same script as Hannity, yet she went viral. This was cause for concern at Fox and management took the opening to cut her loose. Later that week, America began to shut down with Disney World closing, the NBA suspending the season, and Broadway theaters going dark. An internal Fox memo reminded staff that viewers depended on them to stay informed. Not everyone got that memo and continued to support travel, which was unsafe, if not essential. Then on Friday the

13th, a turning point and not coincidentally for the President was reached. Regan was put on hiatus to send a message, she was soon fired outright, but her contract was paid out for silence.

Within a couple of days, talent was reporting from home, and social distancing was of vital importance. Carlson laughed at the change since two days earlier, everyone was "overreacting." Though Fox was changing its tune, a great deal of propaganda was still being spread. Fox talent was reporting predominantly from newly created home studios. The hosts admitted they were lucky as other media companies were cutting jobs. In March, Fox's ratings surpassed February at a record high. Soon after, Fox was accused of being complacent in the death of many Americans because of their coverage. This was directed at Hannity as well. Hannity hired a P.R. firm and lawyer to stop using his coverage against him when others were also soft on the coronavirus around the same time. This continued into April with Fox minimizing the virus and feeding Trump information.

This all resulted in an untouchable cable network and an untouchable politician protected by them. Just before social distancing went into effect, Stelter met with a source to discuss Fox. Though the Murdoch brothers had differing opinions, power would not exchange hands until Rupert died. Until then, Fox was facing a bigger threat. Trump wanted Trump TV, and if not reelected, he had people lined up to bankroll his own network. He would no longer need Fox but be in business against them. Fox had created a monster, and though the chance to rein him in was present at one time, it had been ignored. This made the whole thing even more ridiculous.

Recap of Chapter 6

- Trump wants a network and will create his own if not reelected.

- Trump's response to coronavirus was limited because he was

    distracted.

- Fox was complacent in sharing the truth about coronavirus.

- Even though Fox did not tell America about the true danger of

    coronavirus, they prepared at their studio ahead of time.

- Fox has created a monster in Trump that they can no longer

    control.

Conclusion of "Hoax"

Certain parts of the media are controlled by an unpredictable president. This leads to misinformation for a large portion of the American population. This also upends democracy in that free press is being limited. Radical Republicans are being created, and addiction to Fox News can be at least partially blamed. Until the Fox-Trump alliance (unofficial) is ended, the truth and basic journalistic principles will not be restored on the Network. This is dangerous at worst and ungenuine at best.

Test Yourself on "Hoax"

1. What news network does Stelter currently work for?

2. Who is currently the "Shadow Chief of Staff?"

3. Whose show seemingly prompted Trump to stop air travel to and from China in the wake of coronavirus?

4. Name three people who moved from Fox to White House jobs or related jobs.

5. How did Trump redefine "hoax?"

6. Name three networks called "fake news" by Trump.

7. Who was first sued and fired (resigned) from Fox for harassment?

8. Who took over at Fox upon Ailes' dismissal?

9. Which Murdoch currently runs Fox?

10. What well-known corporation purchased a large portion of the Fox empire?

11. What source did Stelter first think may have been a plant by Fox?

12. Who left Fox in 2017 because he could no longer deal with Trump on the political trail?

13. Who was the "wardrobe enforcer" who ultimately held a high

position at Fox?

14. How much was Bill Shine offered in his severance agreement?

15. What position did Hannity help Shine get with Trump?

Answers for "Test Yourself" Questions

1. CNN

2. Sean Hannity

3. Tucker Carlson

4. Bill Shine, Ben Carson, Bolton, Scott Brown, Lea Gabrielle

5. Hoax was once only associated with something made up and never real. Trump redefined it to represent media stories, most often that did not favorably represent him.

6. CNN, ABC, NBC

7. Ailes

8. Rupert Murdoch temporarily to name a replacement

9. Rupert Murdoch but not as CEO

10. Disney, excluding Fox News

11. Sean Graf

12. Campaign Carl Cameron

13. Suzanne Scott

14. 7 million dollars

15. Bill Shine temporarily served as communications director for less than a year.

Discussion Questions on "Hoax"

1. Did Trump intend on finding a news outlet to take over when he was elected President?

2. Is Trump's obsession with media a help or a hindrance? Explain.

3. Is the term 'hoax' something Trump uses to draw attention away from his own errors? Explain

4. Has Fox inadvertently created a monster in Trump? Explain

5. Do Americans have the ability to separate truth from fallacy when watching the news networks? Why or why not?

6. Has Fox created a cult of radicalized Republicans? Explain

7. Is this book written by a concerned American or a concerned reporter? Explain

8. Can the news ever be truly unbiased? Explain

9. Could coronavirus deaths have been limited by a faster response? How? Would there have been limitations?

10. Should a president be reliant on media for information? Why or why not?

11. How is Hannity standing in opposition to journalistic integrity?

12. Is it appropriate for reporters and staffers to move from Fox to the White House? Why or why not?

13. Is Fox in trouble if Trump starts his own network? Why or why not?

14. Was it wrong for Fox to take coronavirus precautions before telling the general public to do so? Why or why not?

15. Will coronavirus and media coverage and the cover-up help or hinder Trump's chances at reelection? Explain

Editorial Review of "Hoax"

Hoax is a book that serves a singular purpose, to make the connection between Fox News and Trump clear to the general public. Readers will not be able to ignore the clear connections to Trump's talking points, and the various 'favorite' shows he views and records incessantly. Neither will they be able to overlook his almost daily calls to Hannity and others at the Fox network. The trade between Fox and Trump, Trump creating a soft landing for those no longer working at Fox, is undeniable.

The title *Hoax* is about the media and Trump's use of the term to describe what he once called "fake news." This title seems to carry weight among radical Republicans, even if they do not necessarily agree with the current approach Fox is taking. When reviewing the sheer number of changes, especially in personnel, that Fox has undergone, there seems to be a clear issue with who is running the company and who is pulling strings. It may not be possible for Fox to recover credibility among those outside the

audience. Only time will tell.

"Hoax" in a Tweet

Brian Stelter uses his reporting skills to warn Americans about the bias Fox shows toward the sitting President and the dangers it poses to democracy as a whole.

About Your Summarizer

Amanda W. specializes in reading books and text on the toughest of topics and summarizing it in a way that is easily understood by the general public. An avid reader with a passion for sharing on a range of topics, she has transferred her love of teaching and reading into a career of virtual writer and editor on a wide host of topics. When asked what she is up to, her answer is always reading a new book.

THANK YOU FOR FINISHING THE BOOK!

Looks like you've enjoyed it! :)

Please help me reach more readers by taking 30 seconds to write just a few words on Amazon now

Warmly,

wizer Team

Claim Your Unannounced Bonus

Hope you enjoyed reading this summary and discussions wizer book as much as we enjoyed bringing it to you.

Our philosophy is to always delight and over-deliver, so here's one final bonus for you.

If you've enjoyed this book, please leave a review because it will help us reach more readers like you.

If you do, we will rush you 3 valuable bonuses not offered to public:

1. A beautiful, easy to read 1-page recap of all the highlights in this book so you can refer to it over and over (Great for retention!)

2. Ideas on how to implement this book's powerful ideas into your life (As you may agree, it's not what you know, it's what you *keep*)

3. Even more trivia questions to test yourself and your friends!

As you can see, these are going to be an invaluable resource that will accelerate your growth and learning.

Here's what to do to claim it now:

1. Leave a review https://www.amazon.com/review/create-review/error?channel=glance-detail&asin=B08KFLJT19&ie=UTF8&

2. Claim it at http://gowizer.com/reviews

3. Receive your bonus within 24-48 hours!

That's it!

Hope you enjoy your extra bonuses and thank you again for your loyalty with wizer summary and discussions.

See you on the next wizer,

The wizer Team

Made in the USA
Middletown, DE
18 November 2020